FRAMEWORKS OF GEOGRAPHY
DECODABLE GRAPHIC NOVEL

INTRODUCTION TO
CLIMATE
AND
BIOMES

Written by Izzi Howell

Illustrated by Steve Evans

CHERRY LAKE PRESS

WORLD BOOK

a Scott Fetzer company
Chicago

Published in the United States of America by Cherry Lake Publishing Group
Ann Arbor, Michigan
www.cherrylakepublishing.com

Produced in partnership with World Book , Inc.
World Book, Inc.
180 North LaSalle Street
Suite 900
Chicago, Illinois 60601
USA

Illustrator: Steve Evans
Decodable Text Adaptation: Cherry Lake Press

Additional spot art by Shutterstock

Cherry Lake Press is an imprint of Cherry Lake Publishing Group.

Library of Congress Cataloging-in-Publication Data has been filed and is
available at catalog.loc.gov.

Cherry Lake Publishing Group would like to acknowledge the work of the
Partnership for 21st Century Learning, a Network of Battelle for Kids.
Please visit Battelle for Kids online for more information.

Printed in the United States of America

TABLE OF CONTENTS

What Is Climate? 4

What Affects Climate? 6

What Is a Biome? 12

Tropical Rain Forest Biomes............... 14

Temperate Forest Biomes 18

Taiga Forest Biomes 20

Grassy Biomes 22

Dry Biomes 26

Polar Biomes 30

Aquatic Biomes 34

Our Changing World 38

Words to Know 40

There is a glossary on page 40. Terms defined in the glossary
are in type **that looks like this** on their first appearance.
Pronunciations can be found alongside their first appearance.

WHAT IS CLIMATE?

Look at this nice day!

I'm Climate.

You can thank me for the bright sun that you usually find in this place.

I am not the same as weather, which can change each day. It can change each minute!

I need an umbrella!

Climate is weather in a place over a long time. Patterns show up each year.

A place's climate is lots of things. It is how hot or cold it is. It is how much this can change. It is how much sun a place gets.

It is if it rains, snows, or hails. It is how much it rains, snows, or hails. It is how wet the air is. It is how much it storms...

...and wind speed and direction.

Let's meet Wind... Wind is my best pal!

Yes! I play a big role in climates!

Why is it hot and dry in this place...

...but is rainy and foggy by the sea?

Five main things **influence** this.

1. LATITUDE
2. ELEVATION
3. TOPOGRAPHY
4. WATER BODIES
5. WINDS

influence: IN-floo-uhns

INFLUENCE 1

Latitude. Each place has it. It is the spot each place sits between the **equator** and a pole. It is shown in degrees, which you write with this: °. The equator is at 0°. Each pole has a latitude. The North Pole is at 90°N and the South Pole is at 90°S.

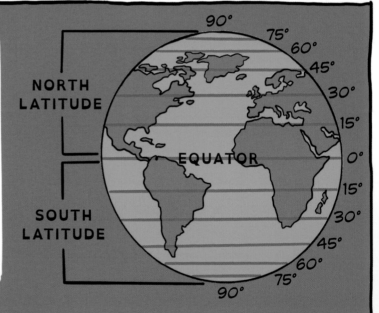

NORTH LATITUDE

SOUTH LATITUDE

EQUATOR

90° 75° 60° 45° 30° 15° 0° 15° 30° 45° 60° 75° 90°

At 0°, the sun's rays shine straight at the land. Such straight rays make it hot. Spots not close to 0° curve away.

latitude: LAT-uh-tood
equator: ih-KWAY-tuhr

6

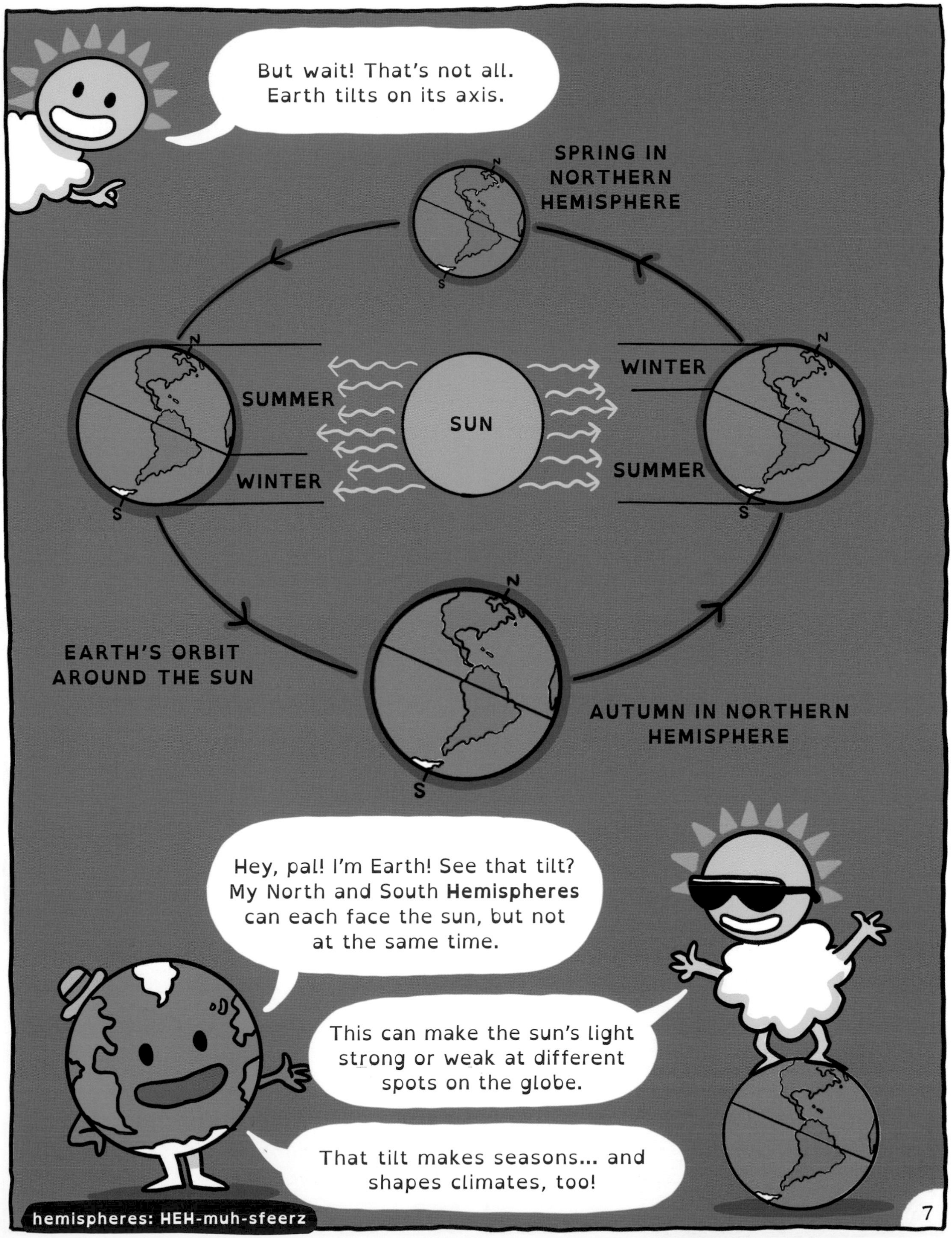

But wait! That's not all. Earth tilts on its axis.
SPRING IN NORTHERN HEMISPHERE
N
S
SUMMER
WINTER
SUN
WINTER
SUMMER
EARTH'S ORBIT AROUND THE SUN
AUTUMN IN NORTHERN HEMISPHERE
Hey, pal! I'm Earth! See that tilt? My North and South **Hemispheres** can each face the sun, but not at the same time.
This can make the sun's light strong or weak at different spots on the globe.
That tilt makes seasons... and shapes climates, too!
hemispheres: HEH-muh-sfeerz

It's much too hot with this coat on! In middle latitudes, temperatures, or temps, change when seasons change. High and low temps in each season stay close each year.

Earth's tilt can change the length of days and nights, too. Day and night can change length with the seasons. Middle latitudes get warm summers with long days. Winters get cold and nights get long.

It's too soon for snow!

Polar winters get cold and do not get much sun. At each pole, the sun will not rise at all in winter.

Polar summers get mild temps and long days. On some days, the sun will not set at all.

It's too bright! I can't sleep!

The sun's rays hit the equator straight on all year long. Its climate is hot at all times. But not at high **elevations**.

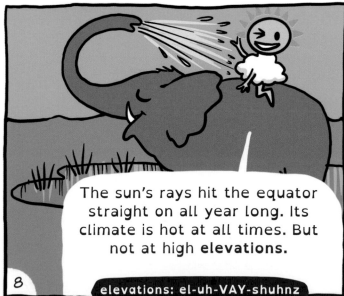

At the equator, day and night last the same length (~12 hours) all year long.

elevations: el-uh-VAY-shuhnz

INFLUENCE 2

Elevation. This is how high each place is above sea level. High heights can make spots colder.

High **plains** and mountain ranges get cold winters. They get snow. Summers stay cool. These spots get lots of wind, too!

This is too much wind!

plains: PLAYNZ

Mountain tops get lots of snow. It stays cold. Snow sits up on top, even when it's hot down at the base.

You will need a face cover like this!

INFLUENCE 3

Topography. Land can change from place to place. Peaks and high land change patterns of wind, rain, snow, and hail in a place.

Clouds drop rain and snow on mountain sides that face the wind.

This dry side is known as a rain shadow.

Air warms up as it flows past the mountain's back side. Clouds fade.

Wet air that went over water cools when it hits steep slopes.

Not much rain or snow drops on the back side.

topography: tuh-PAH-gruh-fee

4

Big seas and lakes shape climate, too. Right, Ocean?

Yes! I can heat and cool land and air. Sea air collects and holds water. That can make wet climates.

In summer, temps in big seas and lakes can't rise as fast as temps on land. It's just too much water to heat up!

Brrrr! That's no joke!

In winter, oceans take more time to get cold than land.

Not bad!

Ocean currents run like huge conveyor belts. They take hot and cold water around the globe.

They take heat at the equator and use it to heat water at high latitudes.

Cold currents at each pole flow at the equator and cool **tropical** spots.

On to the poles with this warm water!

On to the equator with this cool water!

tropical: TRAH-pih-kuhl

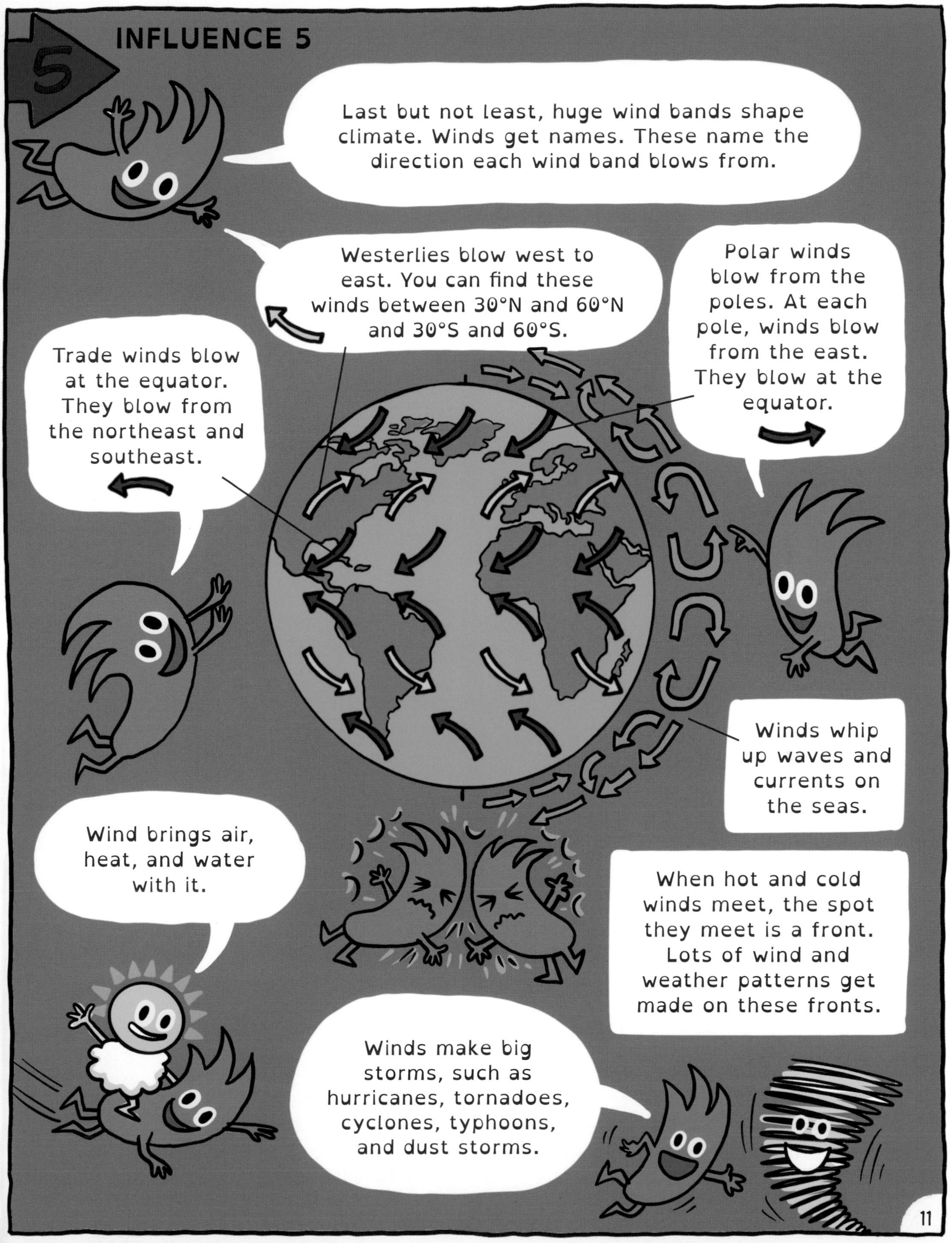
5
INFLUENCE 5
Last but not least, huge wind bands shape climate. Winds get names. These name the direction each wind band blows from.
Westerlies blow west to east. You can find these winds between 30°N and 60°N and 30°S and 60°S.
Polar winds blow from the poles. At each pole, winds blow from the east. They blow at the equator.
Trade winds blow at the equator. They blow from the northeast and southeast.
Winds whip up waves and currents on the seas.
Wind brings air, heat, and water with it.
When hot and cold winds meet, the spot they meet is a front. Lots of wind and weather patterns get made on these fronts.
Winds make big storms, such as hurricanes, tornadoes, cyclones, typhoons, and dust storms.

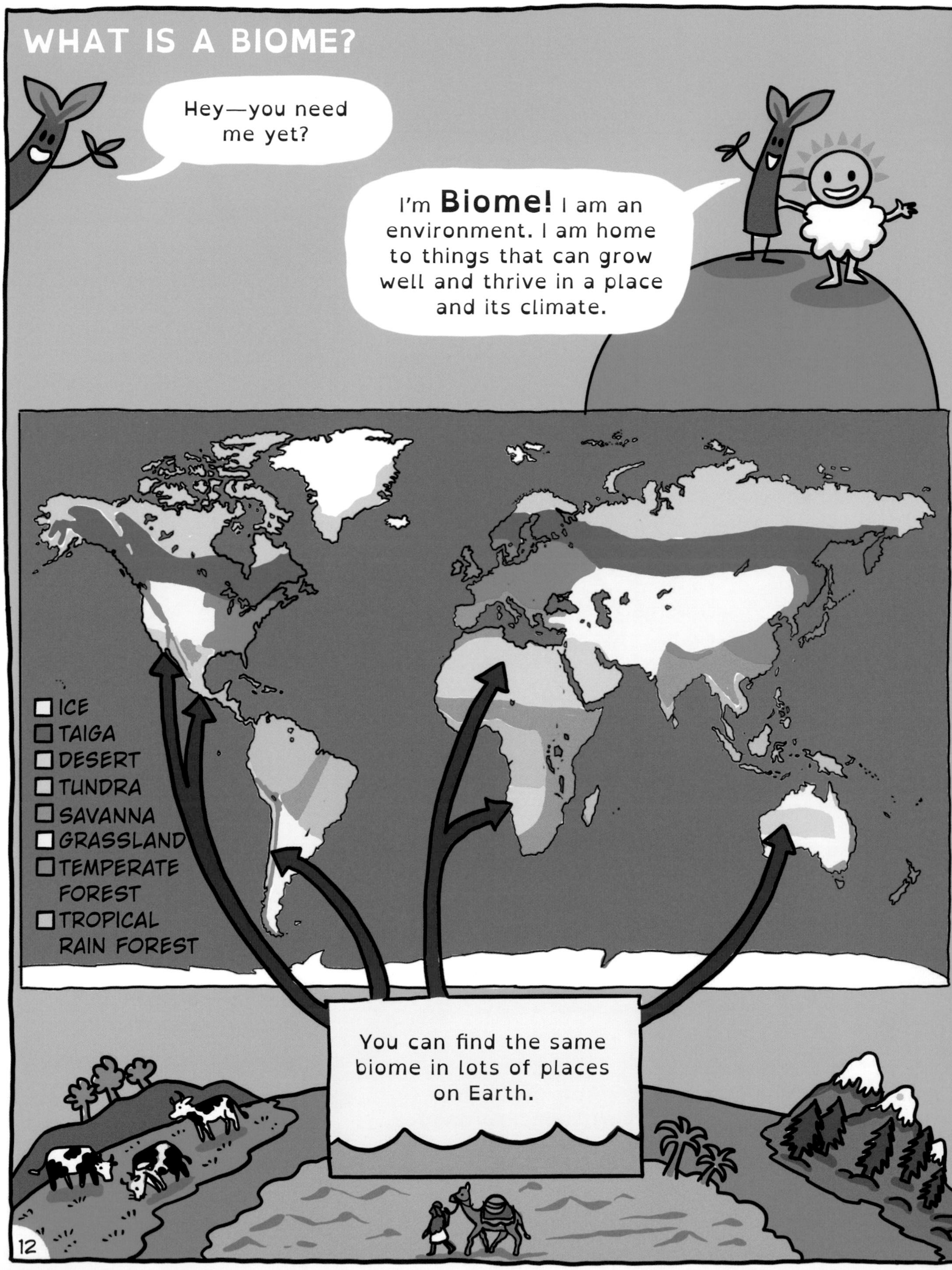

WHAT IS A BIOME?
Hey—you need me yet?
I'm **Biome!** I am an environment. I am home to things that can grow well and thrive in a place and its climate.
ICE
TAIGA
DESERT
TUNDRA
SAVANNA
GRASSLAND
TEMPERATE FOREST
TROPICAL RAIN FOREST
You can find the same biome in lots of places on Earth.

Is that the same as an **ecosystem**?

Nope. It's not. That is each living and nonliving thing in each place, such as sand dunes, and ways they interact.

ecosystem: EE-koh-sis-tuhm

You might find lots of ecosystems in each biome. Did you know that each layer of a rain forest biome has its own ecosystem? It's true!

Each biome type has the same climate. It has the same kinds of living things. Let's look at biome types now!

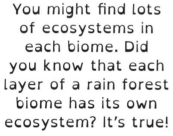

TROPICAL RAIN FOREST BIOMES

Let's look at this place! You can see why it's a rain forest! It sure does rain lots in this place!

This place can get at least 100 inches (254 centimeters) of rain each year. At least it will not drop all at once!

Rain forests boast tropical wet climates—you can find them at the equator. It is hot and wet the whole year.

Plants and trees thrive well with strong rain, high humidity, and hot temps in this place.

The Amazon rain forest is in South America. It is huge! It is the biggest tropical rain forest on Earth. It has 2 million square miles (5.2 million square kilometers) of trees.

Rain forests are **biodiverse**. This means that lots of different plants and animals thrive in these spots.

This snake is not nice!

biodiverse: bye-oh-duh-VERS

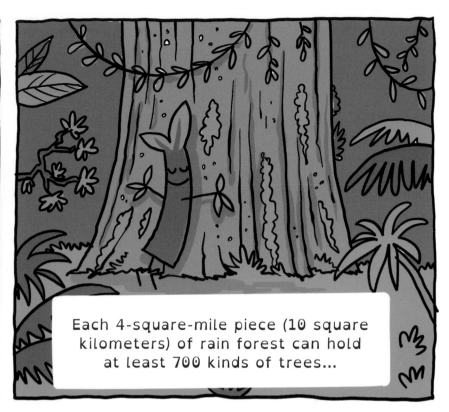

Each 4-square-mile piece (10 square kilometers) of rain forest can hold at least 700 kinds of trees...

...more than 100 types of butterflies...

... and 400 kinds of birds!

Rain forests might hold at least half of all kinds of plants and animals on Earth. That's millions! Biologists find new kinds each day!

This damp, dark forest floor with its dead leaves makes good meals for bugs, worms, rodents, and animals that eat bugs, such as anteaters.

Past that, let's climb up in the damp, hot understory. Flowering trees fill it. It is just right for tree frogs that need to keep their skin damp!

Up, up, up we climb. This is the canopy—tree branches cross and make a roof! Sun and rain can pass through it. It is quite bright, but wet.

The canopy has lots of fruit and nut trees. These make this layer home to the most animals.

deforestation: dee-for-uh-STAY-shuhn

TEMPERATE FOREST BIOMES

This place has lots of trees, too, but it is not a rain forest. A good way away from the equator and tropical spots, you can find these **temperate** forest biomes.

temperate: TEM-pruht

Temperate forests can grow in moderate climates. These climates get a good amount of rain. Seasons change in these spots, too.

Temps in these spots can get hot. They can get cold. Temps change based on the time of year. A place like this will not get temps that are too high or too low and that stay that way for months on end.

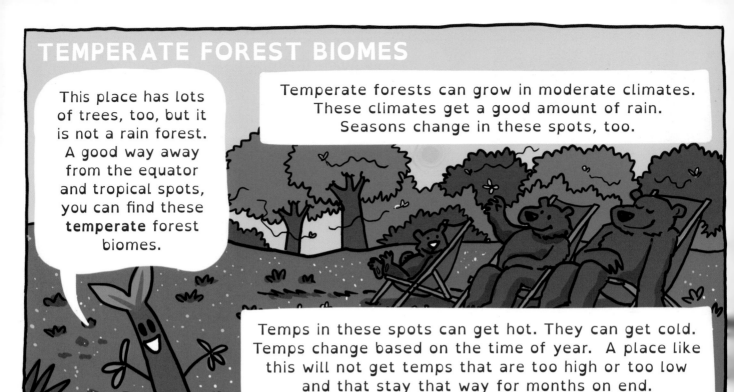

Not too hot, not too cold, just right!

Each animal here has **adapted**. Each year, they make it through high temps, low temps, rain, snow—lots of weather types!

That should last!

Squirrels find nuts in fall and stash them to eat in winter and early spring, when food is tough to find.

adapted: uh-DAP-tuhd

Lots of birds, such as this wood thrush, migrate in fall. They spend winter in a place with more heat and sun.

In spring, these birds take long flights back home when it gets warm.

See you next year!

18

Deciduous trees grow in temperate forests. This kind of tree can fill up some forests. These trees drop leaves in fall. The leaves change colors. Then they fall off.

These trees stay bare through winter.

New leaf buds grow in spring.

Its leaves grow big in time for summer.

Conifer trees grow in temperate forests, too. This kind of tree can fill up other forests. These trees and others like it are evergreen trees.

They change leaves just a bit at a time. They never look bare.

Trees like this grow leaves like needles or scales. Conifers grow seed pods, too. These are cones.

This snow means that it's... winter!

TAIGA FOREST BIOMES

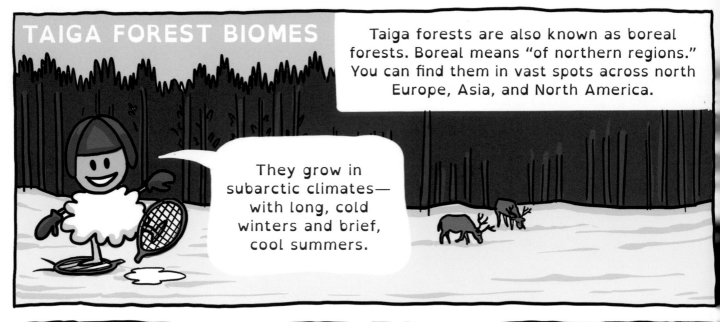

Taiga forests are also known as boreal forests. Boreal means "of northern regions." You can find them in vast spots across north Europe, Asia, and North America.

They grow in subarctic climates— with long, cold winters and brief, cool summers.

It is so cold in these spots that some soil stays frozen at all times. This is known as **permafrost**. It stops water, which then sits on top.

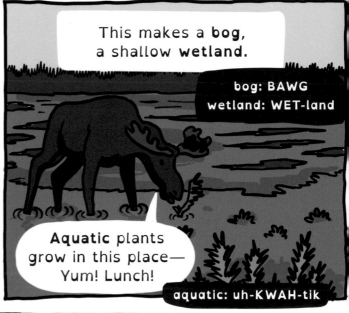

This makes a **bog**, a shallow **wetland**.

bog: BAWG
wetland: WET-land

Aquatic plants grow in this place— Yum! Lunch!

aquatic: uh-KWAH-tik

Lots of conifer trees thrive in these spots. Needle-like leaves will not freeze in cold temps.

Lots of living things fill these biomes. They adapted and can thrive in cold temps. Many animals leave this place when temps get too cold. They trek back when it warms up.

This thick fur coat keeps me snug.

This white coat makes it tough for **predators** to spot me in snow... I hope!

predators: PREH-duh-tuhrs

In the past, both temperate and taiga forests grew on huge swaths of land. They grow on much less land these days.

Back 10,000 years ago, folks started to change the land. They cut trees. They dug up wild plants. Then they grew crops on it.

Deforestation is a big threat, just as it is in rain forests.

Not as much forest is left, and it might not last. Pollution, logging, and development could wipe it out.

We must keep these biomes safe and stop them from disappearing for good.

GRASSY BIOMES

While trees rule forests, grass is the star on the savanna!

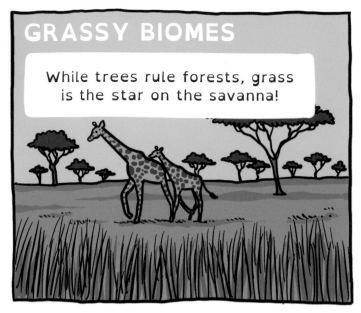

These biomes are also known as tropical grasslands. You can find them between deserts and rain forests. They grow in tropical spots. They cover two-fifths of Africa and big swaths of India and Australia, too.

They stay hot all year. Each has brief wet seasons with rain and then long dry seasons with not much rain.

It's a good thing that you got umbrellas!

In dry seasons, grass will not grow. It dries up and turns brown. Lots of trees lose leaves.

Wildfires sweep through in dry seasons. These fires can, in fact, help life in this place.

They get rid of dead and dying growth.

Fires keep things balanced with big plants (trees and shrubs) and grass.

In rainy seasons, life wakes back up. Grass grows green and trees grow fresh leaves..

New grass shoots grow. Roots stay safe underground while plant stems and leaves burn up. This way, plants survive.

Long time no see!

Huge herds of animals, such as zebras and wildebeest, graze on grass. They trail rains through the African savanna.

Is it nap time yet?

Big predators like lions and cheetahs hunt them.

Mom... mom... let's eat!

People like to take trips here and go on a safari.

They can see how much life this place has.

BIOME TOURS

A steppe is a grassland biome, too. You can find these in temperate climates. These spots sit between tropical and polar zones.

The Eurasian Steppe is huge. It is the biggest on Earth. It goes one-fifth of the way around the globe! It goes from East Europe to Central Asia.

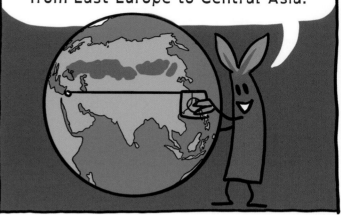

A steppe has a semiarid climate. This means that it will not get much rain—just 10–20 inches (25– 51 centimeters) each year.

Is that it?

Grass can't grow high on steppes. Most plants stay less than 1 foot (30 centimeters) high.

Look at you!

It has a wide temp range. It has hot summers and ice cold winters and cold nights.

A prairie is a wide stretch of flat grassland with long, thick grass and few trees.

Animals such as this pronghorn antelope, prairie dogs, and lots of birds and snakes make this place home.

Look out! That snake bites!

These biomes are temperate.

In these spots, it rains in late spring and early summer. Summers can get too hot and too dry. Winters pass long and cold.

Prairies get more rain than steppes (15–35 inches)!

Rain at last! Drink up!

Prairie grass can grow high. It can grow as big as grown adults!

Is someone in there?

DRY BIOMES

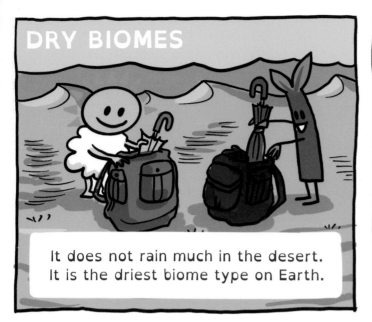

It does not rain much in the desert. It is the driest biome type on Earth.

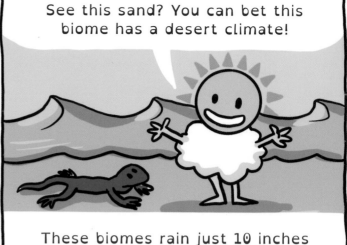

See this sand? You can bet this biome has a desert climate!

These biomes rain just 10 inches (25 centimeters) or less each year.

Most think that deserts get hot, and that is true when the sun is up...

...but at night, temps drop low! Clouds can trap heat. This place has no clouds. As soon as the sun sets, it gets cold quick.

You can find deserts far from the equator. In deserts like this, it gets cold in winter as well.

Deserts are not just flat sand and sand dunes! They can be plains with stones on top, big rocks, cliffs, hills, mountains, and even huge salt flats!

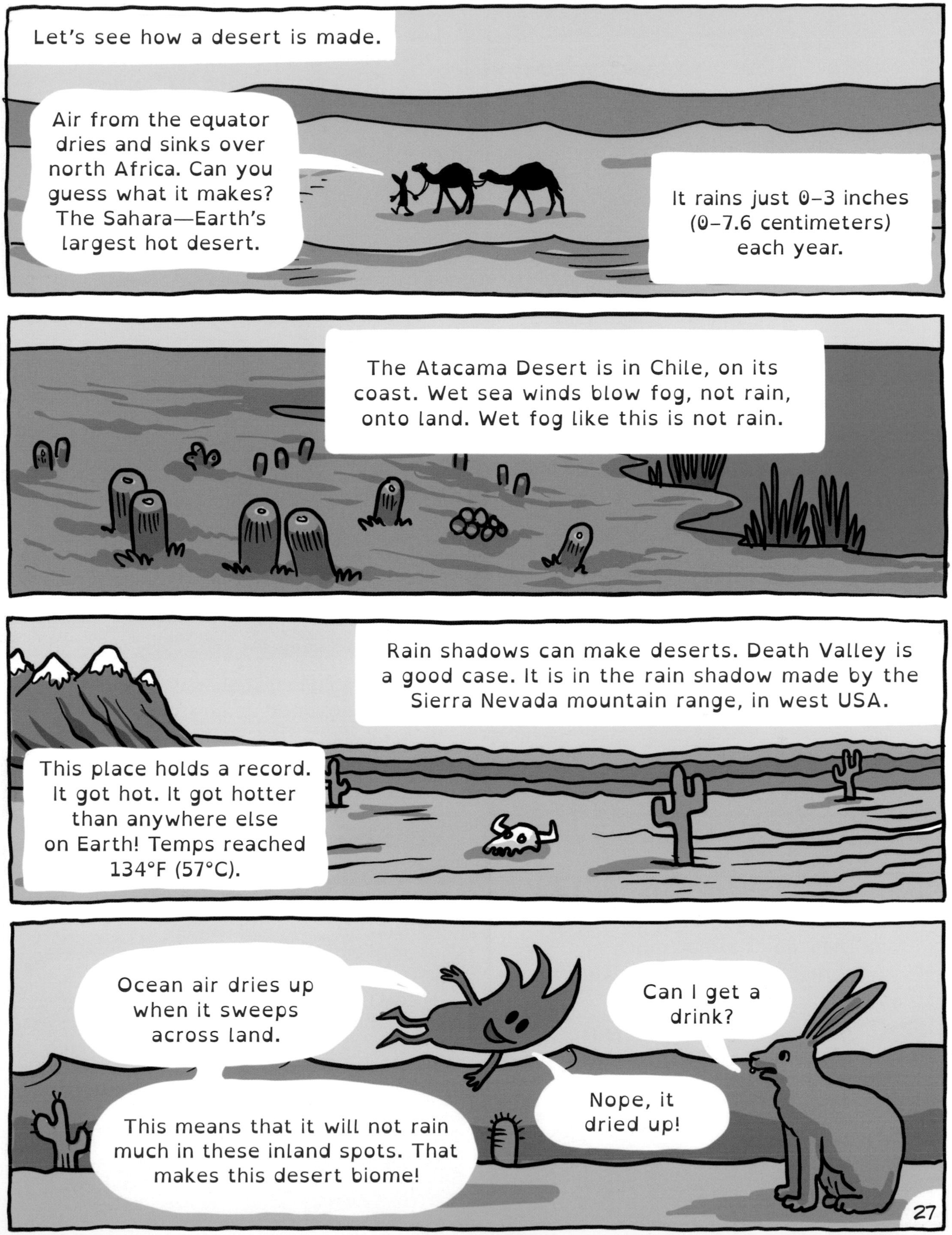
Let's see how a desert is made.
Air from the equator dries and sinks over north Africa. Can you guess what it makes? The Sahara—Earth's largest hot desert.
It rains just 0–3 inches (0–7.6 centimeters) each year.
The Atacama Desert is in Chile, on its coast. Wet sea winds blow fog, not rain, onto land. Wet fog like this is not rain.
Rain shadows can make deserts. Death Valley is a good case. It is in the rain shadow made by the Sierra Nevada mountain range, in west USA.
This place holds a record. It got hot. It got hotter than anywhere else on Earth! Temps reached 134°F (57°C).
Ocean air dries up when it sweeps across land.
This means that it will not rain much in these inland spots. That makes this desert biome!
Can I get a drink?
Nope, it dried up!

You will need hats, fans, and water if you take a trip to the desert.

But desert animals and plants adapt. They deal with hot days and lack of rain in strange and cool ways.

Lots of desert animals are **nocturnal**. It is too hot in the harsh and bright sun. Kangaroo rats hide in holes underground in day time. They leave when the sun sets and it gets cool.

Not yet!

nocturnal: nahk-TER-nuhl

This fox has big ears. It is a fennec fox. Its ears help it keep cool. Blood vessels in them let heat out like huge vents.

This saguaro cactus has roots that reach deep, deep underground. Its roots seek out water. Its thick stem and wax-like skin help store that water it finds and keep it from drying up.

These camels need water, but can survive without it for weeks or months at a time. They get what they need in food. They don't sweat much and save as much water as they can.

Must.... not... sweat...

Underground water can rise up at an **oasis**.

Animals and plants meet at these points to drink and eat.

oasis: oh-AY-suhs

Human activity can wreck lots of biomes. But deserts are expanding. This is due to **desertification**.

When people cut trees and dig up plants, roots can't hold soil in place.

With no roots, wind blows good soil off the land. It is **eroded**. Land then gets dried up. Things can't grow.

This is not a good thing. These spots are not the same as natural deserts. These spots might not have desert climates. Animals and plants in these spots did not adapt. They will not thrive and grow.

No thanks!

You can plant new trees. They will help hold dirt in place. This can help! These trees can make new habitats and food for animals. It's a win-win!

POLAR BIOMES

Brrr! This change in temp is not fun! It was too hot and then it got too cold!

Look at us in this tundra biome!

The Arctic Circle holds most of these biomes. This is a line. It is not real. It is at 66°N.

ARCTIC CIRCLE

Alpine tundras sit on high mountain peaks.

Bah!

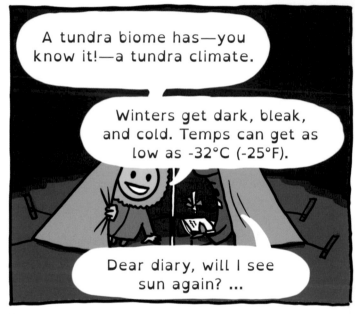

A tundra biome has—you know it!—a tundra climate.

Winters get dark, bleak, and cold. Temps can get as low as -32°C (-25°F).

Dear diary, will I see sun again? ...

Tundra winters get lots of wind!

Summer temps can rise up to 32–50°F (0–10°C). But summer is brief. It lasts just 6–10 weeks. Let's make the most of it!

The tundra is past the tree line. This is the point past which trees can't grow. In fact, tundra means "treeless."

We can see the tree line on mountains, too.

Trees just can't grow in the tundra. Low temps, high winds, and frozen ground make it that way.

Let's head south!

You can still find plants on the tundra. Shrubs and grass grow here. Colorful **lichens** grow, too.

lichens: LYE-kuhns

These plants shoot up quick when temps get mild.

Sun's up! Let's grow, grow, grow!

Shrubs, grass, and lichens are food for tundra animals like musk oxen, caribou, lemmings, and snow geese.

Munch, munch!

Each of those is then food for predators, like Arctic wolves, too!

Is that a juicy musk ox I smell?

The ground in this place is rich in metals, oil, and coal.

People mine and drill to get these things. That wrecks the homes of tundra plants and animals.

More mines here would be a threat to the land. Let's pass laws to keep this place safe for a long time.

Keep it safe!

If you think it's tough on the tundra, let's look at an ice cap! Ice biomes are in polar regions, too.

You can bet that it is quite, quite cold! This climate is an ice climate or ice cap climate.

An ice cap is a glacier—a thick ice sheet that sits on land.

Ice cap biomes are near each pole.

Most of Greenland is in this biome type.

And most of Antarctica has a huge ice cap on top!

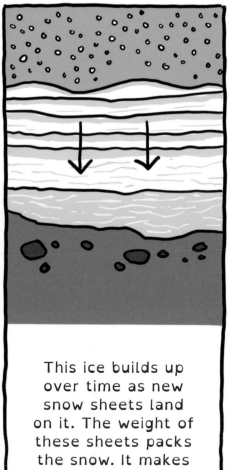

This ice builds up over time as new snow sheets land on it. The weight of these sheets packs the snow. It makes strong ice.

Plants don't grow in this biome. Lots of animals can't get through these tough conditions. But you can find some, such as sheep and musk oxen, at the edge of this land.

Let's not get too close!

You can find ice biomes in a high mountain range, too, such as in the Himalaya and the Andes.

Each has the same climate as ice caps.

AQUATIC BIOMES

Biomes are not just on land! Let's ask my pals if they can guide us!

Hey, it's me—Ocean! I am the largest biome on Earth. You can find me on 71% of it!

I am also known as a marine biome.

Hey, I am Fresh Water! I am in streams, lakes, and ponds.

You can find most of life on Earth in this biome!

You can tell us apart. Salt makes us different.

I hold lots of salt!

I am not salty at all. Humans and lots of other animals drink fresh water. Too much salt would make them sick.

Lots of animals and plants live in water.

Can you show us?

Each aquatic animal has things that help it thrive in this place. Gills let sharks and fish take in oxygen. This is how they breathe...

GILLS

...while aquatic mammals, such as whales, dolphins, and otters, and reptiles, such as sea turtles, must swim back up to breathe.

They can hold their breath for a long time. They can stay underwater and hunt food.

Most aquatic animals have smooth, sleek frames that help them swim fast.

Plants in this place, such as seaweed, need sun to make food, just like plants on land. This means that they must grow close to the surface. Sunlight can't reach deep spots.

Look! Sun... yum, yum!

Can you take us to see some of your ecosystems?

Yes! Let's kick it off with one that we share ...

...an estuary! This is where fresh and ocean water meet.

This water has a bit of salt in it. Not just any plants and animals can thrive in this mix.

Look at this place! It's an underwater forest! But you will not find trees in it. These are giant kelp, a kind of seaweed!

Lots of animals thrive in this place. Sea urchins eat kelp, then sea otters eat sea urchins!

Fish and other animals hide in kelp when things hunt them.